Bible Study Series
for junior high/middle school

THE TRUTH ABOUT
Spiritual Growth

Group

Loveland, Colorado

The Truth About Spiritual Growth

Core Belief Bible Study Series

Copyright © 1997 Group Publishing, Inc.

Credits
Editors: Bob Buller, Debbie Gowensmith, and Lisa Baba Lauffer
Creative Development Editor: Paul Woods
Chief Creative Officer: Joani Schultz
Copy Editor: Janis Sampson
Art Director: Bill Fisher
Computer Graphic Artist/Illustrator: Ray Tollison
Photographer: Craig DeMartino
Production Manager: Gingar Kunkel

Unless otherwise noted, Scriptures quoted from The Youth Bible, New Century Version, copyright © 1991 by Word Publishing, Dallas, Texas 75039. Used by permission.

ISBN 0-7644-0860-7

10 9 8 7 6 5 4 3 2 1   06 05 04 03 02 01 00 99 98 97

Printed in the United States of America.

Bible Study Series
for junior high/middle school

contents:

the Core Belief: ▼Spiritual Growth

Christianity isn't a onetime shot. Regardless of how we become Christians, the quality of our lives on earth and our intimacy with God depends on whether we're seeking to grow spiritually on a daily basis.

Spiritual growth means learning more about God by reading his Word. It also means pursuing holiness—continuing to confess to God our sins and shortcomings and seeking to grow beyond them. As we grow spiritually, we learn to treat others as Jesus would.

Today's young people need to know that Christianity is a vital path, one we walk down our whole lives until we get to that final destination—the place that Jesus has prepared for us.

the ▼Helpful Stuff

the ▼Studies

▼Spiritual Growth as a Core Christian Belief

Teenagers today are very discerning. They're not easily fooled by people who put on spiritual fronts but have little spiritual depth. Unfortunately, teenagers often see people like that in churches today—people who may very well have a true faith in Jesus but who aren't really growing closer to God in their daily lives. Seeing such stagnant Christians can turn kids off to a vital, growing relationship with God.

By understanding the true nature of spiritual growth, your kids can see that a stagnant or hypocritical relationship with God isn't what God wants. Kids can see that God desires a growing, deepening relationship with his children that's exciting and life-changing. Once kids know what's possible with God, they'll be motivated to seek him with all their hearts.

These studies will help your kids understand how spiritual growth deepens their relationship with God and therefore enriches their lives. First they'll take a look at the **busyness** in their lives that prevents them from making a growing relationship with God a priority. They'll learn that with a commitment to God, they'll grow spiritually.

The second study gives kids direction in their struggle to figure out their **self-image.** They'll discover that by looking to Jesus for answers about who they're supposed to be, he will free them to be who they truly are.

In the third study, kids will learn that they can't grow spiritually by themselves—that it takes the **accountability** of family, friends, and themselves to help each other focus on growing closer to God.

Finally, the last study will help kids refocus on spiritual fitness instead of placing a higher priority on **physical fitness.** Parallels between physical and spiritual exercise will help kids learn practical ways to grow spiritually.

Becoming a Christian marks the beginning of a miraculous change that continues to progress right up to the moment of death—and beyond. God never intended teenagers to trust in Jesus for their salvation and then to live out the rest of their lives without God. He wants them to grow in their relationship with him—personally experiencing the grace, mercy, and love of God in ever-increasing measures every day.

*For a more comprehensive look at this Core Christian Belief, read Group's **Get Real: Making Core Christian Beliefs Relevant to Teenagers.***

DEPTHFINDER

HOW THE BIBLE DESCRIBES SPIRITUAL GROWTH

Spiritual growth is a process. Although you become a "new creation" in Christ the moment you believe in him, you're not automatically freed from the tendency to sin. In fact, any Christian who's striving to live for Christ will struggle with the desire to sin. But through the power of the Holy Spirit, you can say no to sin.

Over time, as you continue to choose God's way, you'll become more and more like Jesus. That growth takes place through a combination of allowing the Holy Spirit to lead you in your life and deciding consciously to follow the Holy Spirit instead of your sinful desires.

According to Scripture, spiritual growth occurs as we grow in knowledge, holiness, and intimacy with God (John 16:12-14; Romans 7:14-25; Romans 8:5-16; 2 Corinthians 5:17; Galatians 5:16-25; and 1 John 3:21-24). Let's take a closer look at each of these aspects:

- **Spiritual growth means growing in knowledge.** Before we can make changes in our lives, we have to know what God wants for us. That knowledge comes largely through the study of the Bible. By reading and studying the Bible, as well as other books and materials that are based on biblical principles, we can learn more about God and how he wants us to live. We can also learn from other Christians and from personal experiences with the Holy Spirit. Growing in knowledge is a part of spiritual growth but alone will not result in spiritual growth (Deuteronomy 5:1; Mark 12:24; John 5:39-40; Philippians 1:9-11; 2 Timothy 2:15; and 3:14-17).

- **Spiritual growth means growing in holiness before God.** Holiness involves striving to follow the example of Christ in all we do. Acting on what we learn about God shows we really know and love him. And obeying God—producing the fruit of the Spirit in our lives—is true spiritual growth (Psalm 1:1-2; 119:97-104; Galatians 5:22-23; Ephesians 1:16-17; 5:1-2; 2 Timothy 3:14-17; James 4:4-8; and 1 John 2:3-6).

● **Spiritual growth means becoming like Jesus in the way we treat other Christians.** God doesn't intend for us to function in this world as loner Christians. In the church he gave us brothers and sisters to share our hurts and needs as we struggle to grow through the difficulties of life. Part of that growth involves learning to use the spiritual gifts God gives us through the Holy Spirit. Those gifts are given to Christians to be used for the benefit of the church and those outside the church (1 Corinthians 12; Galatians 6:1-5; 1 Thessalonians 5:11; 2 Thessalonians 1:3-4; Hebrews 10:24-25; and James 5:13-20).

● **Spiritual growth means becoming like Jesus in the way we live in the world.** Once we become Christians, we're no longer to love the world, but we're to love the people in the world. God wants us to care for the poor, the sick, the orphans, the widows, and all those who don't have a relationship with him through Jesus. He wants us to serve him by serving them. He also wants us to let others know how they can have the relationship with him that we do. As we grow in our understanding of who God is and what he has done for us, we will grow in compassion for these hurting people God loves (Proverbs 14:21; Matthew 25:34-45; 28:19-20; James 1:27; and 1 Peter 3:15-16a).

CORE CHRISTIAN BELIEF OVERVIEW

Here are the twenty-four Core Christian Belief categories that form the backbone of Core Belief Bible Study Series:

The Nature of God	Jesus Christ	The Holy Spirit
Humanity	Evil	Suffering
Creation	The Spiritual Realm	The Bible
Salvation	Spiritual Growth	Personal Character
God's Justice	Sin & Forgiveness	The Last Days
Love	The Church	Worship
Authority	Prayer	Family
Service	Relationships	Sharing Faith

Look for Group's Core Belief Bible Study Series books in these other Core Christian Beliefs!

about

Bible Study Series
for junior high/middle school

Think for a moment about your young people. When your students walk out of your youth program after they graduate from junior high or high school, what do you want them to know? What foundation do you want them to have so they can make wise choices?

You probably want them to know the essentials of the Christian faith. You want them to base everything they do on the foundational truths of Christianity. Are you meeting this goal?

If you have any doubt that your kids will walk into adulthood knowing and living by the tenets of the Christian faith, then you've picked up the right book. All the books in Group's Core Belief Bible Study Series encourage young people to discover the essentials of Christianity and to put those essentials into practice. Let us explain...

What Is Group's Core Belief Bible Study Series?

Group's Core Belief Bible Study Series is a biblically in-depth study series for junior high and senior high teenagers. This Bible study series utilizes four defining commitments to create each study. These "plumb lines" provide structure and continuity for every activity, study, project, and discussion. They are:

● **A Commitment to Biblical Depth**—Core Belief Bible Study Series is founded on the belief that kids not only *can* understand the deeper truths of the Bible but also *want* to understand them. Therefore, the activities and studies in this series strive to explain the "why" behind every truth we explore. That way, kids learn principles, not just rules.

● **A Commitment to Relevance**—Most kids aren't interested in abstract theories or doctrines about the universe. They want to know how to live successfully right now, today, in the heat of problems they can't ignore. Because of this, each study connects a real-life need with biblical principles that speak directly to that need. This study series finally bridges the gap between Bible truths and the real-world issues kids face.

● **A Commitment to Variety**—Today's young people have been raised in a sound bite world. They demand variety. For that reason, no two meetings in this study series are shaped exactly the same.

● **A Commitment to Active and Interactive Learning**—Active learning is learning by doing. Interactive learning simply takes active learning a step further by having kids teach each other what they've learned. It's a process that helps kids internalize and remember their discoveries.

For a more detailed description of these concepts, see the section titled "Why Active and Interactive Learning Works With Teenagers" beginning on page 57.

So how can you accomplish all this in a set of four easy-to-lead Bible studies? By weaving together various "power" elements to produce a fun experience that leaves kids challenged and encouraged.

Turn the page to take a look at some of the power elements used in this series.

THE ISSUE: Relationships

Betrayed!

B E T R A Y E D

HELPING KIDS DEAL WITH REJECTION FROM THE PEOPLE THEY LOVE

by Jennifer Carrell

THE POINT:

God is love.

■ Betrayal has very little shock value for this generation. It's as commonplace as compact discs and mosh pits. For many kids today, betrayal characterizes their parents' wedding vows. It's part of their curriculum at school; it defines the headlines and evening news. Betrayal is not only accepted—it's expected. ■ At the heart of such acceptance lies the belief that nothing is absolute. No vow, no law, no promise can be trusted. Relationships are betrayed at the earliest convenience. Repeatedly, kids see that something called "love" lasts just as long as it's

The Study
AT A GLANCE

SECTION	MINUTES	WHAT STUDENTS WILL DO	SUPPLIES
Discussion Starter	up to 5	JUMP-START—Identify some of the most common themes in today's movies.	Newsprint, marker
Investigation of Betrayal	12 to 15	REALITY CHECK—Form groups to compare anonymous, real-life stories of betrayal with experiences in their own lives.	"Profiles of Betrayal" handouts (p. 20), highlighter pens, newsprint, marker, tape
	3 to 5	WHO BETRAYED WHOM?—Guess the identities of the people profiled in the handouts.	Paper, tape, pen
Investigation of True Love	15 to 18	SOURCE WORK—Study and discuss God's definition of perfect love.	Bibles, newsprint, marker
	5 to 7	LOVE MESSAGES—Create unique ways to send a "message of love" to the victims of betrayal they've been studying.	Newsprint, markers, tape
Personal Application	10 to 15	SYMBOLIC LOVE—Give a partner a personal symbol of perfect love.	Paper lunch sack, pens, scissors, paper, catalogs

notes:

● **A Relevant Topic**—More than ever before, kids live in the now. What matters to them and what attracts their hearts is what's happening in their world at this moment. For this reason, every Core Belief Bible Study focuses on a particular hot topic that kids care about.

● **A Core Christian Belief**—Group's Core Belief Bible Study Series organizes the wealth of Christian truth and experience into twenty-four Core Christian Belief categories. These twenty-four headings act as umbrellas for a collection of detailed beliefs that define Christianity and set it apart from the world and every other religion. Each book in this series features one Core Christian Belief with lessons suited for junior high or senior high students.

"But," you ask, "won't my kids be bored talking about all these spiritual beliefs?" No way! As a youth leader, you know the value of using hot topics to connect with young people. Ultimately teenagers talk about issues because they're searching for meaning in their lives. They want to find the one equation that will make sense of all the confusing events happening around them. Each Core Belief Bible Study answers that need by connecting a hot topic with a powerful Christian principle. Kids walk away from the study with something more solid than just the shifting ebb and flow of their own opinions. They walk away with a deeper understanding of their Christian faith.

● **The Point**—This simple statement is designed to be the intersection between the Core Christian Belief and the hot topic. Everything in the study ultimately focuses on The Point so that kids study it and allow it time to sink into their hearts.

● **The Study at a Glance**—A quick look at this chart will tell you what kids will do, how long it will take them to do it, and what supplies you'll need to get it done.

The Bible Connection
The Bible Connection—This is the power base of each study. Whether it's just one verse or several chapters, The Bible Connection provides the vital link between kids' minds and their hearts. The content of each Core Belief Bible Study reflects the belief that the true power of God—the power to expose, heal, and change kids' lives—is contained in his Word.

THE POINT OF *BETRAYED!*:

God is love.

THE BIBLE CONNECTION

1 JOHN 4:7-21 — The Apostle John explains the nature and definition of perfect love.

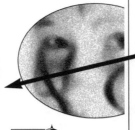

In this study, kids will compare the imperfect love defined in real-life stories of betrayal to God's definition of perfect love.

By making this comparison, kids can discover that God is love and therefore incapable of betraying them. Then they'll be able to recognize the incredible opportunity God off relationship worthy of their absolute trust.

Explore the verses in The Bible Connection mation in the Depthfinder boxes throughout understanding of how these Scriptures conne

LEADER TIP

THE STUDY

DISCUSSION STARTER ▼

Jump-Start (up to 5 minutes) As kids arrive, ask them to thin common themes in movies, books, TV show have kids each contribute ideas for a mast two other kids in the room and sharing sider providing copies of People magazi what's currently showing on television or at their suggestions, write their respon s on new **come up with a lot of great ide s. Even tho ent, look through this list and ry to discov ments most of these theme have in comm

After kids make several su gestions, mention responses are connected w th the idea of betray

● Why do you think etrayal is such a co

Betrayed! 17

LEADER TIP for The Study
Because this topic can be so powerful and relevant to kids' lives, your group members may be tempted to get caught up in issues and lose sight of the deeper biblical principle found in The Point. Help your kids grasp The Point by guiding kids to focus on the biblical investigation and discussing how God's truth connects with reality in their lives.

DEPTHFINDER — UNDERSTANDING INTEGRITY

Your students may not be entirely familiar with the meaning of integrity, especially as it might apply to God's character in the Trinity. Use these definitions (taken from Webster's II New Riverside Dictionary) and other information to help you guide kids toward a better understanding of how God maintains integrity through the three expressions of the Trinity.

Integrity: 1. Firm adherence to a code or standard of values. 2. The state of being unimpaired. 3. The quality or condition of being undivided.

Synonyms for integrity include probity, completeness, wholeness, soundness, and perfection.

Our word "integrity" comes from the Latin word *integritas*, which means soundness. *Integritas* is also the root of the word "integer," which means "whole or complete," as in a "whole" number.

The Hebrew word that's often translated "integrity" (for example, in Psalm 25:21 [NIV]) is *tam*. It means whole, perfect, sincere, and honest.

CREATIVE GOD-EXPLORATION ▼

Top Hats (18 to 20 minutes) Form three groups, with each trio member from the previous activity going to a different group. Give each group Bibles, paper, and pens, and assign each group a different hat God wears: Father, Son, or Holy Spirit.

Depthfinder Boxes—These informative sidelights located throughout each study add insight into a particular passage, word, historical fact, or Christian doctrine. Depthfinder boxes also provide insight into teen culture, adolescent development, current events, and philosophy.

Leader Tips—These handy information boxes coach you through the study, offering helpful suggestions on everything from altering activities for different-sized groups to streamlining discussions to using effective discipline techniques.

---

handout

Holy Profiles

Your assigned Bible passage describes how a particular person or group responded when confronted with God's holiness. Use the information in your passage to help your group discuss the questions below. Then use your flashlights to teach the other two groups what you discover.

■ Based on your passage, what does holiness look like?

■ What does holiness sound like?

■ When people see God's holiness, how does it affect them?

■ How is this response to God's holiness like humility?

■ Based on your passage, how would you describe humility?

■ Why is humility an appropriate human response to God's holiness?

■ Based on what you see in your passage, do you think you are a humble person? Why or why not?

■ What's one way you could develop humility in your life this week?

Handouts—Most Core Belief Bible Studies include photocopiable handouts to use with your group. Handouts might take the form of a fun game, a lively discussion starter, or a challenging study page for kids to take home—anything to make your study more meaningful and effective.

The Last Word on Core Belief Bible Studies

Soon after you begin to use Group's Core Belief Bible Study Series, you'll see signs of real growth in your group members. Your kids will gain a deeper understanding of the Bible and of their own Christian faith. They'll see more clearly how a relationship with Jesus affects their daily lives. And they'll grow closer to God.

But that's not all. You'll also see kids grow closer to one another.

That's because this series is founded on the principle that Christian faith grows best in the context of relationship. Each study uses a variety of interactive pairs and small groups and always includes discussion questions that promote deeper relationships. The friendships kids will build through this study series will enable them to grow *together* toward a deeper relationship with God.

GOING NOWHERE FAST

by Rick Chromey

HELPING KIDS SLOW DOWN TO GROW CLOSER TO GOD

THE POINT:

When you commit to God, you grow spiritually.

■ Kids today are starving spiritually. They sense a deeper meaning to life, and they want to find it. ■ They just don't have the time. ■ Brought up in a fast-paced society where instant gratification is taken for granted, kids ride a bullet train through life. With school, family, friends, and after-school activities, kids' daily planners are full, scheduled to the last minute. ■ When do today's young people "pencil in" time with God? And how can they understand that spiritual growth takes time—a lifetime committed to God? ■ This study will help your kids recognize their need to slow down and invest their time in a lasting

The Study
AT A GLANCE

SECTION	MINUTES	WHAT STUDENTS WILL DO	SUPPLIES
Learning Game	10 to 15	BUILDIN' ON THE WORD—Stack cups on their Bibles, walk, and read Scripture at the same time.	Bibles, paper, pens, magazines, paper cups, scissors, tape, table
Creative Bible Discovery	25 to 30	SEEDS OF CHANGE—Creatively explore the parable of the seed and the soils and apply what they learn to their lives.	Bibles, "Seed and the Four Soils" handouts (p. 23), pens
Life Change	10 to 15	THIRSTY HEARTS—Cut dried sponges into heart shapes, then dip the sponges into water to make them expand.	Bibles, dried sponges, airtight plastic bag, scissors, markers, paper cups, water

notes:

When you commit to God, you grow spiritually.

THE BIBLE CONNECTION

MATTHEW 6:19-34	Jesus exalts spiritual "treasure."
MATTHEW 13:1-9, 18-23	Jesus explains the story of the seed and the four soils.

I n this study, kids will play a game to help them realize how busyness can crowd out a relationship with God. Then they'll creatively explore the parable of the four soils and evaluate which soil best describes their own spiritual growth.

Through these experiences, kids can discover that rather than investing time in pursuits that eventually fade away, they can commit their lives to God and invest in something eternal—their spiritual growth.

Explore the verses in The Bible Connection; then examine the information in the Depthfinder boxes throughout the study to gain a deeper understanding of how these Scriptures connect with your young people.

LEADER TIP for The Study

Whenever you tell groups to discuss a list of questions, write the list on newsprint and tape the newsprint to a wall so groups can discuss the questions at their own pace.

BEFORE THE STUDY

For the "Buildin' on the Word" activity, set an eight-foot-long table along one wall of your meeting room. If you'll have more than twelve students at your meeting, set two tables along the same wall.

Make a copy of the "Seed and the Four Soils" handout (p. 23) for each student.

Gather one four-by-eight-inch cellulose sponge (available at grocery stores) for every four students in your class. Cut the sponges into four pieces, each measuring one-by-two inches. Preheat an oven to two hundred degrees or less. Place the sponges on the oven rack, and let them "bake" for eight to ten minutes. When sponges are thoroughly dried, smash them as flat as possible. If you live in a humid area, you may need to wait and do this just prior to teaching the lesson. Store the dried sponges in an airtight plastic bag.

For every four students, label a paper cup with the phrase "Commitment to God," and then fill each paper cup with water.

THE STUDY

LEARNING GAME ▼

Buildin' on the Word
(10 to 15 minutes)

Before students arrive, set out paper, pens, old magazines, paper cups, scissors, and tape. When everyone has arrived, say: **Today we're going to discuss how busy our lives can be and how our busyness affects our relationship with God. To start, take a piece of paper and a pen; then write down the top five situations, people, or things that consume your time—for example, family, school, video games, movies, television, pets, or friends.**

Next search the magazines I've provided for pictures that represent each of your "time consumers." For example, you might find pictures of skateboards, books, or groups of friends. If you can't find just the right pictures, you might find words or letters to spell out your time consumers. Cut out the pictures, words, and letters that best represent your time consumers, and tape them to paper cups, one time consumer per cup.

After five minutes, have each person stack his or her cups inside each other and place the stack on the table you set up before the study. Then have kids gather on the opposite side of the room and open their Bibles to Matthew 6:19-34. Say: **We're going to play a game using the cups. When I say "go," read aloud Matthew 6:19-34. As you read, walk to the table, take one cup from your stack, and place the cup somewhere on your open Bible. Then, still reading aloud, return to this end of the room and touch the wall. After you've touched the wall, walk back to the table, take another cup from your stack, and place it on your Bible. You may put one cup on top of the other if you choose, but you may not stack your cups inside each other. Keep reading the Bible passage aloud as you walk to and from the table, placing your cups on your Bible until you've retrieved all five of them. If you have a "cup crash," that's OK. Just put the cups you've already retrieved back on your Bible and continue with the game. If you come to the end of the Bible passage before you have all five cups, read the passage over again.**

Make sure everyone understands the game, and then say: **Ready? Go!**

Allow kids to play until each has successfully stacked all five cups on his or her Bible or when the group is having more cup crashes than progress. Then have kids form foursomes to discuss these questions:

● **What was the hardest part of this game? the easiest part? Why?**

● **How was trying to balance your cups like trying to balance all the activities in your life? How was it different?**

● **How were the cup crashes like when all your commitments make demands on you at the same time? How were they different?**

DEPTH FINDER
UNDERSTANDING THESE KIDS

How committed are your young people to God? If your students are like the Christian kids surveyed at a major Christian youth event, then...

- almost nine out of ten of them attend church and/or youth group three or more times a month,
- nearly seven in ten feel it's important to share Christ with their friends,
- less than half pray daily,
- four out of ten strongly agree that their Christian beliefs influence their daily decisions,
- one-quarter of them spend at least four hours a month in volunteer service, and
- about two out of ten read their Bibles every day.

Despite some of these low numbers, nearly three-quarters of these Christian teenagers believe that their friends see them as "growing stronger" in their faith.

Christian young people want to grow in their faith, yet (like most of us) they struggle with doing the actions that can bring them closer to God. Use this study as well as one-on-one time with your students to help them invest in their spiritual growth.

(Adapted from GROUP Magazine, February 1995.)

● **How easy was it to read the Scripture after you'd stacked cups on your Bible?**

● **How was this game like the way your time consumers affect your relationship with God? How was it different?**

● **How important is your relationship with God when you're trying to handle these other demands?**

Say: **Today we'll discuss how we get so busy and how our commitments to so many activities distract us from growing close to God. In the end, you'll discover that you bear the fruit of your commitments and that when you commit to God, you grow spiritually.**

CREATIVE BIBLE DISCOVERY ▼

Seeds of Change
(25 to 30 minutes)
Have groups remain together. Hand each student a pen and a copy of the "Seed and the Four Soils" handout (p. 23). Say: **We're going to explore a Bible story about growing spiritually. Before we begin, pray in your groups that God will use this story to teach you what he wants you to learn. You may pray aloud or silently.**

When groups have finished praying, instruct group members to stand with their backs to each other, forming a square. Then have kids link elbows with the people on both sides of them and push against the rest of the group with their legs. While groups do this, read aloud Matthew 13:1-4, 19. When you've finished reading the passage, have groups sit down to discuss the questions and Bible passages under the "Hard Ground" section of the "Seed and the Four Soils" handout.

After five minutes, have each group form a circle. Instruct group members to turn so each person's right shoulder faces the center of the circle, to join right hands and raise them above their heads, to lift their right feet, and to stand tiptoe on their left feet. While groups do this, read aloud Matthew 13:5-6, 20-21. Then have groups sit down to discuss the questions and Bible passages under the "Rocky Ground" section of the handout.

After five minutes, have groups stand in their own circles again. Instruct group members each to gently place his or her hands around the neck of the person on his or her left. As groups do this, read aloud Matthew 13:7, 22. Then have groups sit down to discuss the questions and Bible passages under the "Thorny Ground" section of the handout.

After five minutes, have each group come up with a silent cheer such as doing the "wave." As groups do their cheers, read aloud Matthew 13:8, 23. Then have groups sit down to discuss the questions and Bible passages under the "Good Ground" section of the handout.

After five minutes, have groups discuss these questions:

● **How would you complete the sentence at the bottom of the handout? Why?**

● **What does it mean to "produce fruit" in your life?**

● **Based on what you've learned from this study, how does being a busy person affect your spiritual growth?**

Say: **In the Bible story we just read, three of the four soils produced a plant, but only one produced fruit. It's the same for people. Many of us may hear God's truth, but we don't allow it to go deeply into our hearts and change us. When life troubles us, we turn to the familiar and tangible—things we recognize that we think can comfort us. Or we get so busy trying to make it through life that we don't grow and change after hearing God's truth. We don't bear the fruit God wants us to bear.**

The only way to produce lasting fruit in life is to follow God with everything you have in you. <u>When you commit to God, you grow spiritually.</u> The deeper your roots are in God, the greater your fruits will be in life.

LIFE CHANGE ▼

LEADER TIP
for Thirsty Hearts

If you don't have time to bake the cellulose sponges before the study, flattened, dry sponges are also available at craft or grocery stores.

Thirsty Hearts (10 to 15 minutes) Have kids remain in their foursomes. Distribute a dried sponge to each student and scissors and a marker to each foursome.

Say: **The sponge I handed you represents your heart, so cut your sponge into a heart shape. Then, using the marker, write your name or initials in the middle of the heart shape.**

Have groups discuss these questions:

● **How hard was it to cut your heart shape? Why?**

● **Why was the sponge hard? How did it get that way?**

● **How is your sponge heart like your real heart? How is it different?**

● **How might busyness make your heart hard?**

When groups have finished discussing the questions, give each group a water-filled paper cup labeled "Commitment to God." Say: **Sometimes when we allow our lives to become so busy that we have no time to reflect or relax, our hearts become hard like your sponges. But God can soften our hearts, and when he does, we can grow spiritually.**

In a moment, you'll dip your sponge heart into the water. As you do so, watch how your sponge changes. Think of how the water changing your sponge is like God changing your heart when you commit to him. Invite kids to dip their sponge hearts into their cup of water. As they do, read aloud Matthew 13:23.

"But what is the **seed** that fell on the **good ground?** That **seed** is like the person who hears the teaching and understands it. That person **grows** and **produces** fruit, sometimes a hundred more, sometimes sixty more, sometimes thirty more."

Matthew 13:23

Have groups discuss these questions:

● **How did your sponge heart change as you dipped it into the water?**

● **How was the way the sponge changed like the way God can change your heart when you commit to him? How was it different?**

● **Squeeze your sponge heart. How is the water flowing from your sponge like what happens to your heart when you commit to God? How is it different?**

● **Do you want to grow spiritually? Why or why not?**

● **How might you commit to God so you'll grow spiritually?**

Invite groups to share their answers to the above questions. Then have each student move to a separate spot in the room. Say: **I'm going to say a sentence for you to complete. After I say my part of the sentence, pray about how you'd complete it.**

Say: **An area in my life that tends to "choke" my relationship with God is...**

After thirty seconds, have kids pray about their responses to this statement: **To grow spiritually, I must help my roots grow strong. One way I can start doing this is...**

After three minutes, have kids return to their foursomes to express any personal decisions they've made. Then have group members tell each other "fruits" they see in each other; for example, "Juan, I see God's love in your life, especially in how you give your time to needy people."

Before kids leave, pray: **Dear God, thank you for wanting us to grow closer to you. Please help us grow roots deep in you. Thank you for causing us to grow spiritually when we commit to you.**

the Seed AND the Four Soils

"The Hard Ground"
(Matthew 13:1-4)

1. What does Jesus say the hard ground represents (verse 19)? What eventually happened to the seed?

2. How was your physical pose similar to the hard ground and the type of person it represents? How was it different?

3. Read these Bible passages about people who fit into this category: Pharaoh (Exodus 10:24-29) and King Agrippa (Acts 26:24-28).

Based on these passages, what are three qualities of this type of person?

4. How might living a busy life contribute to someone being like hard ground?

5. Do you know anyone who fits this description? Have you ever fit it? When?

"The Rocky Ground"
(Matthew 13:5-6)

1. What does Jesus say the rocky ground represents (verse 20-21)? What eventually happened to the seed?

2. How was your physical pose similar to the rocky ground and the type of person it represents? How was it different?

3. Read these Bible passages about people who fit into this category: King Saul (1 Samuel 15:17-23) and Judas Iscariot (Luke 22:1-6).

Based on these passages, what are three qualities of this type of person?

4. How might living a busy life contribute to someone being like rocky ground?

5. Do you know anyone who fits this description? Have you ever fit it? When?

"The Thorny Ground"
(Matthew 13:7)

1. What does Jesus say the thorny ground represents (verse 22)? What eventually happened to the seed?

2. How was your physical pose similar to the thorny ground and the type of person it represents? How was it different?

3. Read these Bible passages about people who fit into this category: King Solomon (1 Kings 10:23-25; 11:9-10) and the rich man (Luke 18:18-25).

Based on these passages, what are three qualities of this type of person?

4. How might living a busy life contribute to someone being like thorny ground?

5. Do you know anyone who fits this description? Have you ever fit it? When?

"The Good Ground"
(Matthew 13:8)

1. What does Jesus say the good ground represents (verse 23)? What eventually happened to the seed?

2. How was your physical pose similar to the good ground and the type of person it represents? How was it different?

3. Read these Bible passages about people who fit into this category: Daniel (Daniel 6:1-5) and Joseph (Genesis 39:21-23).

Based on these passages, what are three qualities of this type of person?

4. How might living a busy life contribute to someone being like good ground?

5. Do you know anyone who fits this description? Have you ever fit it? When?

The **soil** that best represents *my* present relationship with *God* is...

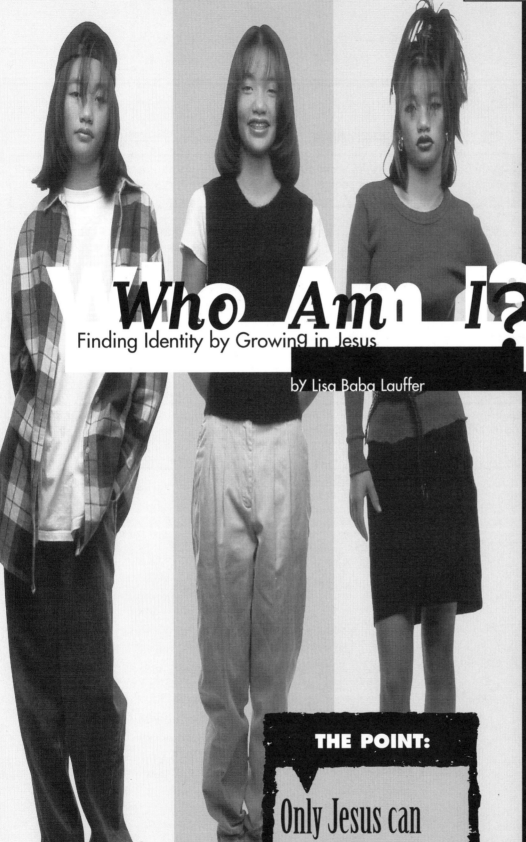

Who Am I?

Finding Identity by Growing in Jesus

by Lisa Baba Lauffer

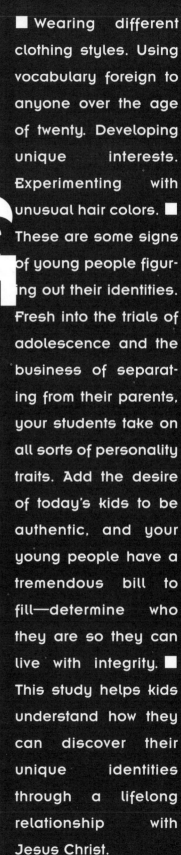

■ Wearing different clothing styles. Using vocabulary foreign to anyone over the age of twenty. Developing unique interests. Experimenting with unusual hair colors. ■ These are some signs of young people figuring out their identities. Fresh into the trials of adolescence and the business of separating from their parents, your students take on all sorts of personality traits. Add the desire of today's kids to be authentic, and your young people have a tremendous bill to fill—determine who they are so they can live with integrity. ■ This study helps kids understand how they can discover their unique identities through a lifelong relationship with Jesus Christ.

THE POINT:

Only Jesus can free you to be yourself.

The Study
AT A GLANCE

SECTION	MINUTES	WHAT STUDENTS WILL DO	SUPPLIES
Creative Opener	up to 5	GREAT NAMES—Discuss the origins and meanings of their names.	Large rock, large paper bag
Bible Discovery	15 to 20	A ROLLER COASTER LIFE—Demonstrate the ups and downs of Peter's life by "riding" a roller coaster.	Bible, "Peter: A Roller Coaster Life" handout (p. 33)
	10 to 15	FEELING LIKE PETER—Explore how Peter fulfilled the identity Jesus gave him.	Bibles, pens, paper
Self-Discovery	15 to 20	TWO SIDES TO MY STORY—Create body collages that express who they are now and who they want to be in the future.	Large sheets of newsprint, magazines, glue, scissors, markers
Closing	up to 5	A SUCCESS STORY—Hear an example of a student who found his identity in Christ.	Supplies from the "Great Names" activity

notes:

Only Jesus can free you to be yourself.

THE BIBLE CONNECTION

MATTHEW 16:15-18   Jesus gives Simon the name "Peter," reflecting Simon Peter's true identity as a "rock" of the church.

ACTS 2:37-41   Luke describes how Peter boldly lives up to his name by sharing the gospel with strangers.

I n this study, kids will examine how to develop their identities. They'll explore Scriptures describing how Simon Peter discovered his true identity through his relationship with Jesus Christ.

Through this experience, kids can discover that the only way to find their true identity is by developing a relationship with Christ.

Explore the verses in The Bible Connection; then examine the information in the Depthfinder boxes throughout the study to gain a deeper understanding of how these Scriptures connect with your students.

BEFORE THE STUDY

Put a large rock into a large paper bag. Make sure the bag is strong enough to hold the rock.

Make one photocopy of the "Peter: A Roller Coaster Life" handout (p. 33).

For the "Two Sides to My Story" activity, cut one eight-foot length of newsprint for each student. Then in each sheet of newsprint, cut a hole in the center large enough for a student to put his or her head through it.

LEADER TIP
for The Study

Whenever groups discuss a list of questions, write the list on newsprint and tape it to a wall so groups can discuss the questions at their own pace.

THE STUDY

LEADER TIP

for Great Names

Before the study, go to the library and check out books on the origin of names. When doing the "Great Names" activity, allow kids to use the books to explore the meanings of their names. Then have kids discuss these questions with their partners:
● Does the meaning of your name according to these books fit who you are? Explain.
● Has finding the meaning of your name helped you discover your true identity? Explain.

LEADER TIP

for The Study

Some kids in your group may not have a relationship with Jesus, but after this study they may want to start one. Be available to your students during and after the study to help them begin a life-long relationship with Jesus Christ.

CREATIVE OPENER ▼

Great Names (up to 5 minutes)
When your students have arrived, have them form pairs to discuss these questions:
● **Who gave you your name, and why did they give it to you?**
● **Do you know the meaning of your name? If so, what is it?**
● **Do you have a nickname? If so, how did you get it?**
● **What does your nickname mean?**
Invite students to tell the meanings of their partners' names and nicknames and the stories of how their partners got these names. Then place the paper bag in front of the group and ask:
● **Can anyone tell me what's in this bag? If so, don't say what it is.**
● **If you don't already know what's in the bag, how could you figure it out?**
Then say: **I'm going to tell you what's in this bag, and you can choose whether to believe me. I won't lie to you about what's in this bag, but since I'm not going to show the object to you right away, you just have to trust that I'm telling you the truth.**
Have pairs discuss these questions:
● **What's your reaction to not knowing what's in the bag?**
● **What's your reaction to trusting the leader to tell you what's in the bag?**
● **How is trusting the leader to tell you what's in the bag like trusting other people or circumstances to tell you what your true identity is?**
● **Where have you looked to find your true identity?**
When pairs have finished their discussions, say: **I have a large rock in this bag. This rock represents the new name that Jesus gave to Simon, one of his disciples. Jesus changed Simon's name to Peter, and the name "Peter" means "rock."**
Ask:
● **Why do you think Jesus gave Simon a name meaning "rock"?**
● **What do you think a person whose name means "rock" would be like?**
After several kids respond, say: **Today we're going to look at how this name change affected Simon Peter. As Simon Peter built his relationship with Jesus Christ, he discovered that he was a new person with a new purpose. And today you'll discover how only Jesus can free you to be yourself. Right now you can't see what's in the bag; you have to trust that I'm telling you the truth about the bag's contents. In the same way, Peter had to wait to experience his true identity; he had to trust that Jesus was telling him the truth about who he was. And you have**

DEPTHFINDER
UNDERSTANDING NAMES IN THE BIBLE

In biblical times, a name held great significance; it described the essence of a person's character. Thus parents carefully chose a child's name. Wrapped up in the name were the parents' hopes—what their child would become and how he or she would behave. In addition, the role of naming a person was powerful and expressed dominion or ownership over that person.

Changing someone's name implied a change in that person's personality and purpose. So when Jesus changed Simon's name to Peter, he was signifying the kind of person Peter would become (strong and stable) and his new mission as the foundation of the church. Jesus also expressed his power over and possession of Peter as his own—his beloved, his friend, and his servant (The Zondervan Pictorial Encyclopedia of the Bible).

to trust that as you build your relationship with Jesus through prayer and Bible study, he'll tell you the truth about who you are.

BIBLE DISCOVERY ▼

A Roller Coaster Life (15 to 20 minutes)

Say: **We're going to study about Peter's life, but before we do, let's go on a roller coaster ride.** Have kids sit in two single file lines facing you and pretend to buckle up their "seat belts" for the ride. Tell them to follow your hand motions, acting as if they really were on a roller coaster ride. For example, when you move your hand to your right, your students should lean to their left. When you move your hand down, your students should lean forward, scream, and even raise their arms if they wish!

When your students are ready, begin the ride. Use your hand to indicate the slow climb up the first hill, big drops, left and right turns, and corkscrew turns.

When the "ride" is over, ask:

● **Is your life ever like a roller coaster? Explain.**

After a few students have responded, say: **Life was like a roller coaster for Simon Peter—he had a lot of ups and downs. But ultimately he figured out who he was and where he was going.**

We're going to listen to some excerpts about Peter's life. As you hear each passage read, pretend you're on the roller coaster of Peter's life. Was his life going uphill? downhill? around a curve? straight? Use your roller coaster motions, just as you did earlier, to indicate how you think Peter's life went at each stage. When the ride is rough, hold on tight! Here we go!

Have three student volunteers take turns reading the Bible passages listed in the "Peter: A Roller Coaster Life" handout (p. 33), and have the rest of the group act out the roller coaster ride.

LEADER TIP
for A Roller Coaster Life

To allow your student volunteers quick access to the Bible passages during this activity, mark the passages with slips of paper or self-stick notes before your meeting.

LEADER TIP
for A Roller Coaster Life

Your students may use different roller coaster motions as your student volunteers read the passages. That's OK. Allow kids their own interpretations of Peter's situations. At the end of the "ride," ask:

● Why did we have different reactions to what happened to Peter in these Bible passages?

● How was each of us moving in different directions like each of us finding our own identity? How was it different?

After Peter's roller coaster ride, have kids form trios to discuss these questions:

● **How was the roller coaster of Peter's life similar to the roller coaster of your life? How was it different?**

● **How do you think Peter felt when Jesus told him he was a "rock"?**

● **How do you think Peter felt during his roller coaster life, knowing that Jesus expected him to be a rock?**

● **How did Peter's relationship with Jesus impact Peter's ability to be a rock?**

● **Do you think Jesus has revealed your identity to you? Explain.**

● **How might a growing relationship with Jesus help you discover your true identity?**

Say: **We've just taken a fun look at Peter's life. But now we're going to delve more deeply into a couple of Scriptures to discover how Peter's relationship with Jesus freed him to be himself and how only Jesus can free you to be yourself.**

Feeling Like Peter (10 to 15 minutes)

Have students form groups of four, and give each group a sheet of paper and a pen. Have groups assign one of these roles to each group member: a Reporter who'll share the group's answers with the rest of the class, a Reader who'll read the Bible passages, a Recorder who'll write the group's answers, and an Encourager who'll make sure all group members participate in the discussion. Then have foursomes discuss these questions:

● **Read Matthew 16:15-18. Have you ever been in a situation like Peter's when someone told you what they thought you'd become? If so, what did that person say, and how did you feel?**

● **Read Acts 2:32-33, 36-42. What happened after Peter finished speaking?**

● **How did Jesus' statement about Peter in Matthew 16:15-18 help explain what Peter did in the Acts passage?**

● **Have you ever accomplished something that someone else encouraged you to do? If so, how did you feel?**

● **How might Jesus free you to be yourself?**

When groups have finished their discussions, have the Reporters share their group's answers. Then ask:

● **How was your group giving you a role like Jesus showing you your true identity? How was it different?**

● **How was carrying out your role like fulfilling the identity Jesus gives you? How was it different?**

Say: **Peter was a real guy. He had good moments and bad moments. But when Peter discovered Jesus' true identity—the Christ who gives us all eternal life—Peter found his own identity as well. This didn't happen all at once—it happened as Jesus and Peter got to know each other.**

In the same way, as you develop a relationship with Jesus, he'll show you who you're meant to be. Only Jesus can free you to be yourself. In the next activity, you'll discover how.

SELF-DISCOVERY ▼

Two Sides to My Story

(15 to 20 minutes) Give each student one of the eight-foot lengths of newsprint you cut before the study. Have kids fold their newsprint in half, make a crease, then unfold it again. As they do this, set out magazines, glue, scissors, and markers.

Say: **We're going to create some fun and wacky collages that show who we are and who we'd like to become. On your piece of newsprint, create this collage that you will wear. On one side of the fold mark, put any pictures or words that describe who you are right now. You can glue pictures or words from the magazines or create your own words or images using the markers. Include anything that describes your interests, personality, activities, or relationships. On the other side of the fold mark, do the same thing, except describe who you'd like to be in the future.**

When kids have finished, have each person put his or her head through the hole to create a "sandwich board" with the "present" flap in front and the "future" flap in back. Then have students go around the room and look at one another's collages. Have kids find partners and point to one positive thing on their partners' collages that expresses an aspect of their partners' true identities.

Then have pairs discuss these questions:

● **How has Jesus freed you to be who you are today?**

● **How might Jesus free you to become all you're meant to be in the future?**

● **What's one thing you can do this week to allow Jesus to reveal your identity to you?**

When pairs have finished their discussions, have students take off their collages and write a short prayer on the future side, asking Jesus to free them to be themselves.

Say: **You now have collages of who you are and what you'd like to become. As you look at them, remember that <u>only Jesus can free you to be yourself.</u>**

LEADER TIP
for A Success Story

If you have a great story of a local junior higher who displayed his or her identity in an extraordinary way, consider telling that person's story instead of Trevor's story.

CLOSING ▼

A Success Story (up to 5 minutes)

Before beginning this section, make sure you have the paper bag with the rock inside. Say: **You may still wonder what your identity is. As you develop a relationship with Jesus Christ over your lifetime, he'll show you the truth about yourself for today and for your future. Only Jesus can free you to be yourself.**

Here's a story about someone your age who discovered the truth about his identity. Several years ago, an eleven-year-old boy named Trevor was watching television. He saw pictures of homeless people wandering through his hometown of Philadelphia. Trevor went to his parents and asked if he could take food and blankets to some of those people—right at that moment!

His parents tried to reason with him that they could do it another day. But Trevor knew that Jesus cared about those people and wanted him to do something for them. Finally, he convinced his parents to take him downtown. The experience of helping the homeless so influenced him and his family that Trevor continued to help those needy people. He enlisted friends to help, and eventually a number of homeless shelters sprang up around Philadelphia, all managed and organized by a boy your age who cared.

Trevor's relationship with Christ helped him see clearly what he needed to do. What about you? Who does Jesus want you to become? What does he want you to do with your life?

Take the rock out of the paper bag and say: **Just like Peter, when you discover Jesus Christ, you discover who you are and what your purpose in this world might be. Will you influence the world like Trevor? It might be less dramatic, but every one of you can discover your purpose if you choose to follow Christ. Only Jesus can free you to be yourself.**

Peter: A Roller Coaster Life

Have three students take turns reading aloud the following Bible passages while the rest of your group indicates where Peter is on the roller coaster of his life.

● **Matthew 4:18-20**—Jesus calls Simon Peter and his brother Andrew to follow him.

● **Matthew 14:25-29**—Simon Peter challenges Jesus to command him to walk on water.

● **Matthew 14:30-31**—While walking on water, Simon Peter becomes afraid and begins to sink.

● **Matthew 16:15-18**—Jesus gives Simon Peter the name "Peter," declaring Peter's true identity as the "rock," the foundation on which Jesus will build his church.

● **Matthew 16:22-23**—Jesus calls Peter "Satan."

● **Matthew 26:31-33**—Jesus says that his disciples will betray him, but Peter claims he will stand firm.

● **Matthew 26:34**—Jesus declares that Peter will betray him three times "before the rooster crows."

● **Matthew 26:73-75**—The rooster crows, and Peter cries as he realizes he's betrayed Jesus three times.

● **Acts 2:37-41**—Peter shares the gospel with strangers.

We're All in This Together

THE POINT:

Being accountable can help you and others grow spiritually.

Why We Need Each Other to Become More Like Christ

by Pamela J. Shoup

■ It often seems that people who have money or clout or the right allies are not accountable for their actions when they do something wrong. Movie stars, sports celebrities, politicians—the rich and famous—often get away with crimes or moral missteps because they hire the savviest lawyers and because their adoring public supports them. ■ What kinds of examples are they for your teenagers? You and their parents are trying to teach them to be accountable for their actions and to learn from the consequences of their choices. ■ Integrity. Responsibility. Courage of convictions. Moral character. Strength. Speaking out on behalf of what's right. These are attributes that strengthen ties with God and foster spiritual growth. You want your teenagers to demonstrate them in every aspect of their lives. ■ But teenagers need help. They need good examples in their daily lives to balance the lack of accountability displayed by so many public figures. They need others to encourage them and to keep them in line, to ask them the tough questions about their thoughts, attitudes, and actions. They need friends, family members, and youth leaders prodding and encouraging them to grow spiritually. They need each other. ■ In this study, teenagers will learn what it means to be accountable to themselves, to one another, and to God—and how accountability will help them and others grow spiritually.

The Study
AT A GLANCE

SECTION	MINUTES	WHAT STUDENTS WILL DO	SUPPLIES
Action Opener	15 to 20	THE GAME OF LIFE—Play a game in which their decisions affect their partners' ultimate success.	Construction paper, markers, tape, pennies, index cards, pencils, and a watch or timer
Bible Exploration	15 to 20	SIN: THEN AND NOW—Discuss sin and accountability by Saul and David in the Old Testament, and modern day rapper Snoop Doggy Dogg, then share those stories in a unique way.	"Sin and Accountability" handout (pp. 44-46), paper sacks, and a variety of objects
Real-Life Situations	10 to 15	PRACTICING ACCOUNTABILITY—Role play situations from the "Game of Life" activity and talk about being accountable to God as well as to families and friends.	Bible, tape, construction paper squares from the "Game of Life" activity
Interactive Closing	5 to 10	BUDDY SYSTEM—Make a commitment to be accountable to a partner.	Bible, construction paper slips, pens or markers, newsprint, tape

notes:

Being accountable can help you and others grow spiritually.

THE BIBLE CONNECTION

1 SAMUEL 15	Samuel confronts King Saul about his disobedience to the Lord. Saul lies and rationalizes his actions, which eventually leads to his destruction.
2 SAMUEL 11; 12:1-19	David sins with Bathsheba; then God sends the prophet Nathan to confront David, who admits his sin.
HEBREWS 10:24-25	This passage teaches that Christians need to show love and encouragement to each other to help each other grow spiritually.

I n this study, kids will learn what accountability is and how their actions affect their own and other people's spiritual growth. They'll explore biblical and modern-day examples of accountability to learn how others have or have not been accountable.

By doing this, kids can learn to foster spiritual growth in themselves and others by taking responsibility for their actions, by being good examples for each other, and by motivating each other to be accountable.

BEFORE THE STUDY

For the "Game of Life" activity, write the following four situations on four different-colored sheets of construction paper. Number each square clearly.

1. A friend has a bunch of used stereos, and you could make some quick money by selling them to other friends. Do you do it?

2. You're at a party where everyone is drinking beer. Do you join in, figuring that it won't hurt because your parents won't know?

3. Your friend has been sick and is not prepared for a test. She's whispering behind you, asking for test answers. Do you help her out?

4. Your mom asks you to watch your baby sister while she goes to a meeting. Do you tell your little brother to take care of the baby, figuring that everything will be fine as long as you're still in the house?

Tape the four squares to the floor, scattered around the room.

For the "Sin: Then and Now" activity, make a photocopy of the "Sin and Accountability" handout (pp. 44-46), and cut apart the three sections. Prepare three paper sacks (six if you have a large group) so each contains five items kids can use to tell the stories of Saul, David, or Snoop Doggy Dogg. You may use similar or different items for each group.

THE STUDY

ACTION OPENER ▼

The Game of Life (15 to 20 minutes)

After teenagers have arrived, gather them together, and say: **Today we're going to play a game about life. The best part about this game is that you get to have a partner who will help you along the way.**

Explain to kids that they will follow the life-size game board you taped to the floor before the study. Have kids find partners and line up single file in pairs. Give each pair a penny, an index card, and a pencil, and have them number their cards one through four.

Say: **You have five minutes to go to all four squares.**

To travel, you must link arms, flip a penny, and move to a new square only on "heads." There cannot be more than one pair on each square at a time. You have to move fast so everyone has a chance to go to each square. When you get to an open square, read the question and write either "yes" or "no" at the corresponding number on your index card. You and your partner must agree on the answer. Then link arms, and flip your penny; if you get "heads," quickly move to another open square. If you flip "tails," have your partner flip the penny, and take turns flipping until one of you gets "heads." When you're finished, sit over here (designate a space) **with your partners. Go!**

Send the first four pairs, and start timing with a watch or timer. As pairs finish, encourage new pairs to run into the game. After five minutes, call "Stop!"

Gather teenagers together, and have them sit with their partners in groups of four or six. If you have a small group, you may debrief together rather than breaking into groups. Say: **Let's see what kinds of answers you have to these life situations.** Read aloud each question, and have teenagers discuss in their groups what they chose to do in each case and why. After a minute or two on each question, have kids share what they think would be the wise decision and why. For instance, if someone says that the electronic equipment in question number one could be stolen, then you could ask, "What might be the consequences of selling stolen electronics equipment?"

Continue with each question, discussing choices and possible consequences for poor choices. For question number two, consequences could include losing their parents' trust, getting kicked off a sports team, making themselves sick, or injuring themselves. A poor choice for the third situation could result in an automatic "F" on a test. For the fourth situation, a poor choice could result in the baby getting into something she shouldn't and getting hurt. Tell kids to write, "We chose wisely" or "We chose poorly" for each number after the discussion.

LEADER TIP

for The Game of Life

If you have a large group, you may have to allow more time for kids to get to all four squares. However if not everyone gets to play because of some pairs' indecisiveness, kids can still learn from the experience. If this happens in your group, during the debriefing following the game, ask kids who didn't get to finish how it felt to be penalized because of someone else's actions. Ask the other kids how it affected them that not everyone got to finish because of their actions.

If you have fewer than ten kids in your group, send all pairs out at once and call time before five minutes is up if everyone is finished.

DEPTHFINDER
UNDERSTANDING YOUR TEENAGERS

When it comes to teaching your teenagers to be accountable, you first have to know that they understand the difference between right and wrong.

Josh McDowell writes in Youth Ministries magazine (November/December 1995), "Our children are being raised in a society that has largely rejected the notions of truth and morality, a society that has somewhere lost the ability to decide what is true and what is right. Truth has become a matter of taste; morality has been replaced by individual preference."

Today's generation of youth has set new records for dishonesty, disrespect, sexual promiscuity, violence, suicide, and other pathologies, McDowell says, because they have lost their "moral underpinnings"—they don't seem to know right from wrong. In past generations, "a clear understanding of what was right and wrong gave society a moral standard by which to measure crime and punishment, business ethics, community values, character, and social conduct...It provided a cohesive model that promoted the healthy development of the family, united communities, and encouraged responsibility and moral behavior."

Seventy percent of today's youth don't believe anything can be defined as right or wrong. They claim that absolute truth does not exist, that all truth is relative.

McDowell believes that "if our youth are going to learn to determine right from wrong, they must know what truths are absolute and why. They need to know what standards of behavior are right for all people, for all times, for all places. They need to know what determines truth—and why."

Teenagers' beliefs about truth affect their behavior, their choices, and their attitudes. A survey by McDowell shows that failing to embrace truth as an objective standard that governs teenagers' lives will make them

- thirty-six percent more likely to lie to their parents,
- forty-eight percent more likely to cheat on an exam,
- two times more likely to get drunk,
- two times more likely to steal,
- three times more likely to use illegal drugs, and
- six times more likely to attempt suicide.

In his book *Right From Wrong*, McDowell explores practical ways to identify what truths are absolute and how to tell kids why. When you choose an issue to discuss or address, be prepared to answer questions about *why* something is wrong. And remember to attack immoral principles but not people. Use Scripture to help kids seek the truth.

McDowell says, "We can turn our youth, families, and churches around—one person at a time."

Then gather everyone together, and ask:

- **Did any of you convince your partner to make a wise choice? an unwise choice?** Invite kids to comment on specific situations.

- **How might your choices in real life affect those around you?**

- **Accountability means being responsible for one's actions. How do you feel you were accountable in the choices you made during this game?**

Say: **When we're accountable, we try to make choices God would want us to make. And if we make poor choices, we accept the** consequences of those choices. As a result, we grow spiritually.

In our game, some of you did well because of your partners. That happens in real life, too. We all need to help each other be accountable to ourselves, our friends, our families, our teachers and classmates, and especially to God. Being accountable can help you and others grow spiritually.

When you grow spiritually, you have a closer walk with God. Spirituality is a special closeness to God that you demonstrate in the way you live your life. What kinds of things do you think you might do differently as you grow spiritually?

Say: Let's explore some stories in the Bible and in real life about people who sinned and were held accountable for their actions.

BIBLE EXPLORATION ▼

Sin: Then and Now

(15 to 20 minutes) Divide your group into three smaller groups (six groups if you have a large class), and give each group a photocopy of one section of the "Sin and Accountability" handout (pp. 44-46).

Say: Follow the directions on your handout, which are to read the story, discuss the questions, and then act out or tell your story to the entire group using the items in these bags. Give each group a bag of items that you prepared before the study. Allow groups about five minutes to prepare; then have each group retell its story using the items in the bag.

After each group has shared its story, ask:

● Why do some people feel they're not accountable for their actions? Can you give some examples?

● Who do you think of when you think of someone who has integrity, good character, or the courage to stand up for what is right? Why?

● How can you help one another live with integrity, good character, and accountability every day?

● What happens when we refuse to be accountable?

● How can being accountable to each other and to ourselves help us grow spiritually?

● How can you be accountable to God?

Say: Just as David, Saul, and Snoop Doggy Dogg sinned, we all sin, and we all need other people to help keep us on the right path. Being accountable can help you and others grow spiritually. You need your friends and your families to help you by encouraging you to examine your own lives, your attitudes, and your actions. We all need each other. And just as sin separates us from God, learning to be accountable for our actions will bring us closer to God. Let's practice some situations that show how we might be accountable.

DEPTHFINDER
UNDERSTANDING THE BIBLE

There are many parallels in the Old Testament stories of Saul and David, yet the endings to their stories turn out very differently due to their actions—and their accountability.

Let's look at a few of the similarities:

● Saul was the first king of Israel; David was the second king of Israel.

● Both men were very successful in their youth. When Saul was still a young man, Samuel recognized him as God's choice as the future king of Israel; later Saul became a popular military hero. David killed the Philistine giant, Goliath, with just a sling and a stone, which made him popular in King Saul's court and with the people.

● Both were strong, talented, attractive, and had appealing personalities.

● A prophet guided and counseled each king. Saul owed everything to Samuel, but the two disagreed about Saul's role, and Samuel refused to have anything more to do with Saul. David, as a boy, was anointed by Samuel as the one God chose to lead Israel. Later, God sent Nathan to hold David accountable for his sin with Bathsheba. Nathan stayed loyal to David in later years and warned him of a plot against Solomon, David's son and the future king.

● Both Saul and David became powerful leaders and then were confronted with temptations that commonly come with success. Scripture describes how each succumbed to temptation.

But the two kings dealt with their sins in significantly different ways. When Samuel confronted Saul, he didn't repent. Instead, he gave excuses and told lies, which led to shame, dishonor, and his eventual destruction.

When Nathan confronted David, he admitted his guilt. He repented, was punished, and was redeemed. Christ the Savior was born into David's lineage.

Your teenagers need to learn to become mutually accountable. Don't encourage them to go into a "prophetic mode" like Nathan or Samuel and just hold others accountable. They need to be accountable to themselves and others, too.

(Sources: The Zondervan Pictorial Encyclopedia of the Bible and Janice Shaw Crouse, "Leadership: Working from the Inside Out," Vital Speeches of the Day, July 15, 1994.)

REAL-LIFE SITUATIONS ▼

Practicing Accountability (10 to 15 minutes)

For this activity, take the construction paper squares from the "Game of Life" activity, and post them on the wall where everyone can read them. Say: **We're going to role play these situations to practice being accountable or holding someone else accountable. Find a partner, and choose one of these situations or make up your own if you'd like. First, each of you choose a role in your situation, and act out the situation with your partner. For example, you can pretend to be taking a test, and one can ask the other for the answers. One partner should then advise the other one about how to be accountable or responsible in the situation. When you're finished, we'll have some of**

you share your role-plays with the whole group. Give teenagers a few minutes to develop their role-plays. Then ask for several volunteers to act out with the whole group.

Ask:

● **What did it feel like to hold someone else accountable? to be held accountable by someone else?**

● **What makes it difficult to be held accountable or to hold someone accountable? How can you make it easier?**

Say: **Let's read a passage from Scripture together.** Open a Bible to Hebrews 10:24-25, and read it aloud or have a volunteer read it aloud. Ask:

● **What does this passage say about how you should treat other people? about what you should do for yourself to prepare for the Judgment Day?**

● **Can you be an independent person and still be accountable for your actions? can you be independent and still grow spiritually?**

Say: **God tells us that <u>being accountable can help you and others grow spiritually.</u>** Ask:

● **How can we help each other show love to one another? do good deeds?**

By being accountable to one another, our families, our friends, our teachers, and to God, we can grow spiritually. As we practice love and Christian kindness, we can learn to overcome sin or temptation. As we grow spiritually, we also need to set aside time to be accountable to God—to sit and listen to God. Let's take a few minutes to do that.

Find a space in the room where you can be by yourself to pray, to listen to God, and to think about areas in which you can grow spiritually by being responsible for your actions. For example, think about some problem sins or about disciplining yourself spiritually. Give kids a few minutes of silence. Then pray together this prayer or one of your own: **Heavenly Father, we ask for strength to deal with tough issues and to make wise decisions. We ask for your guidance as we support and encourage each other. Help us show good character and integrity in all we do to grow closer to you and to model Christian lives and Christian love. In Jesus' name, amen.**

LEADER TIP for Buddy System

To save time, you can write Hebrews 10:24 on the construction paper slips before class.

INTERACTIVE CLOSING ▼

Buddy System (5 to 10 minutes)

Say: **Today we've learned that <u>being accountable can help you and others grow spiritually.</u> Let's think of some positive ways to keep each other accountable in various areas of our lives.** Have kids share ideas such as prayer, phone calls, encouragement, or confrontation. Let kids be as specific as they want to.

Say: **Let's close with making a commitment to be accountable to**

a partner. Have kids choose same-sex partners. If you have an uneven number of kids, make one group a trio. Say: **With your partner, share ways in your life you believe you are accountable or responsible.** Pause while kids share. Say: **Now identify an area in your life in which you need to be more accountable—maybe doing your homework or getting better grades, being more responsible at home, or making better decisions about friends or activities.** Pause while kids share. Say: **Now make a commitment to pray for each other and discuss how you might help each other stay on track as you grow in your spiritual lives. Then pledge confidentiality not to talk about this with anyone other than your partner.**

When everyone is finished, gather kids together. Have each person share aloud to the group a way in which his or her partner is a responsible or an accountable person.

Distribute construction paper slips and pens or markers to the group. Copy Hebrews 10:24 on a sheet of newsprint, hang the newsprint where everyone can see it, and have each student write the verse on the slip of paper. Then have each student write the name of his or her accountability partner. Tell kids to use the slips as bookmarks or to tack them to the wall in their rooms so they will see them often.

LEADER TIP

for Buddy System

Make "partner sharing" an ongoing part of your youth meetings. Have kids take a few minutes at the beginning or end of each meeting to meet with their partners and check on each other's progress in areas of accountability and spiritual growth.

DEPTH FINDER

HELPING YOUR TEENAGERS GROW SPIRITUALLY

Spiritual growth means a closer walk with God. As people grow spiritually, they learn to overcome sin and temptation, to pray regularly, to read and study the Bible regularly, to love God and others, and to generally take responsibility for their actions and the consequences of those actions.

Teenagers want to belong and to be accepted, so spiritual growth is often easier for teens when friends accompany them in their walk with God.

Teenagers also need good role models, so this might be a good time for you as a youth leader to examine your own spiritual life.

In his book *Spiritual Growth in Youth Ministry*, J. David Stone defines spirituality as "an articulate closeness to God demonstrated in the life that you live. You accept God's gift of life and respond to God in the way that you live with others."

For adults, Stone suggests starting a spiritual growth program with specific goals and objectives. Write out your program, its specific goals, and the steps to take to achieve those goals. Balance your personal program with prayer, study, acting out your faith, and evaluation. You can even form a share group with other youth workers. Or find a spiritual partner to help you keep your ministry Christ-centered and to occasionally ask *you* the tough question: "How is your walk with God?"

Saul's Sin

Read the following story from 1 Samuel 15 as a group; then discuss the questions below.

Samuel, prophet and advisor to King Saul of Israel, delivered a message from the Lord to Saul. The Lord told Saul he would punish the city of Amalek for barring the way when the Israelites were coming from Egypt to Canaan. He told Saul to attack Amalek and to kill all men, women, children, babies, cattle, sheep, camels, and donkeys.

Saul gathered his soldiers and went to the city of Amalek and set an ambush. But first he warned the Kenites to withdraw so he wouldn't have to destroy them. Saul then had all the Amalekites killed but took their king, Agag, alive; Saul also kept the best of the sheep, cattle, and lambs.

Then the Lord spoke to the prophet Samuel, saying, "I am sorry I made Saul king, because he has stopped following me and has not obeyed my commands." Samuel went to meet Saul, but Saul had gone to Carmel where he erected a monument in his own honor. Samuel found Saul, and Saul said, "May the Lord bless you! I have obeyed the Lord's commands." But Samuel heard the sheep and cattle, and Saul told him they were spared from Amalek to sacrifice to the Lord. Samuel confronted Saul, asking him why he had disobeyed the Lord instead of exterminating all of Amalek's citizens and animals. Saul rationalized his decision, repeating that he did obey the Lord and that he had only spared the king and the best animals.

Samuel told Saul that the Lord had rejected him as a ruler because of his disobedience. Saul asked forgiveness, but Samuel repeated, "You rejected the Lord's command, and now he rejects you as king of Israel."

Samuel killed the Amalekites' king, Agag, as the Lord had commanded; never again, as long as Samuel lived, did he see Saul.

- How was King Saul tempted in this passage?
- How did Saul disobey the Lord?
- How did Samuel keep Saul accountable to God?
- How did Saul handle his sin when Samuel confronted him? Did he accept responsibility for his actions? Did he tell the truth?
- How did the Lord punish Saul?
- From this story, what were some of Saul's character traits that led to his destruction?
- How did Saul's actions affect his spiritual growth?

Prepare to retell the story of Saul's sin using the objects in your bag.

David's Sin

Read the following story from 2 Samuel 11 and 12:1-18 as a group; then discuss the questions below.

One evening, from the roof of his palace, King David of Israel saw a beautiful woman. He found out that her name was Bathsheba and that she was the wife of Uriah the Hittite, who was away fighting in a war. David had Bathsheba brought to him, had sexual relations with her, and then returned her to her house. Soon Bathsheba sent David a message that she was pregnant. David ordered that Uriah be sent to the front lines of a battle where the fighting was fierce. Uriah was killed as David had hoped. When Bathsheba had finished mourning, David had her brought to his house, where she became his wife and gave birth to their son.

The Lord sent Nathan the prophet to David to confront him about his sin with Bathsheba and the death of Uriah. Nathan said, "So why did you ignore the Lord's command? Why did you do what he says is wrong? You killed Uriah the Hittite with the sword of the Ammonites and took his wife to be your wife! Now there will always be people in your family who will die by a sword, because you did not respect me."

Then David said to Nathan, "I have sinned against the Lord." Nathan told David the Lord had forgiven his sin but that his newborn son would die. Despite David's prayers and fasting, the baby died. However, David was a successful king, his son Solomon became a successful king, and Jesus Christ was born from David's descendants.

- How was King David tempted in this passage?
- How did David disobey the Lord?
- How did Nathan keep David accountable to God?
- How did David handle his sin when Nathan confronted him? Did he accept responsibility for his actions? Did he tell the truth?
- How did the Lord punish David?
- From this story, what were some of David's character traits that led him to be a great king?
- How did David's actions affect his spiritual growth?

Prepare to retell the story of David using the objects in your bag.

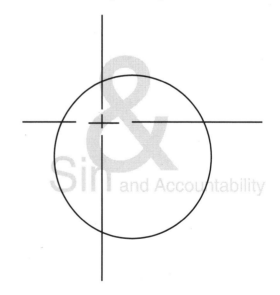

Sin and Accountability

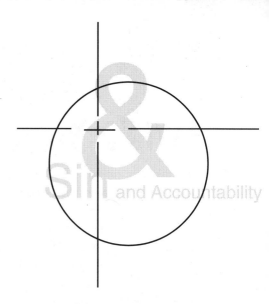
Snoop Doggy Dogg's Sin

Read the following story as a group; then discuss the questions below.

"Gangsta rapper" Snoop Doggy Dogg (Calvin Broadus) was twenty-two years old in 1993 when he and his bodyguard, McKinley Lee, were charged with the murder of Philip Woldemariam, a twenty-year-old Los Angeles gang member.

Lee shot and killed Woldemariam from the passenger seat of a car driven by Snoop after rival gang members exchanged gang signs and verbal insults. Snoop's star was on the rise; he had begun recording his first rap album. He surrendered to police after appearing on the MTV awards as a presenter.

Two and a half years later, a jury found that Lee and Snoop acted in self-defense, and they were found not guilty of murder.

Friends of Woldemariam first insisted he was unarmed but later admitted that a friend removed the gun from the body of the dying Woldemariam to improve the case against Snoop and Lee.

After the trial Snoop's dad, Vernall Varnado, said, "Everybody has a wake-up call in life, a test that makes you or breaks you. Mine was Vietnam. This trial was Snoop's wake-up call."

Snoop said, "A lot of people follow me and respect me. Now I'm gonna step up and handle my position, as far as trying to be the role model I tried to deny at the beginning of my career. I was a follower. Now I look at myself as a leader."

- How was Snoop Doggy Dogg tempted?
- What was Snoop Doggy Dogg's sin?
- Did he show that he was accountable for his actions? Why or why not?
- How might Snoop and his friend McKinley Lee have kept each other accountable?
- Do you think Snoop was found "not guilty" because he was a famous rapper?
- How do you think Snoop might live his life differently because of this experience?

Prepare to retell the story of Snoop Doggy Dogg using the objects in your bag.

The Total Package

The Total Package

Helping Kids Balance Physical and Spiritual Fitness

super sports-hero guy ———→

by Steve Saavedra

■ Anorexic adolescent girls modeling the latest fashions. Celebrities endorsing beauty products. Scanty preteens selling jeans on billboards. Today's youth are bombarded with the message that physical appearance has every-thing to do with popularity, happiness, and success. As a society, we worship athletes. We embrace cosmetic surgery. ■ Our society looks good on the outside, but it's rotting on the inside. We exercise our physical bodies while our spiritual lives waste away. ■ Junior highers want to fit in, and they think they have to look good to fit in. It's easy for them—and all of us—to neglect the soul in favor of primping the body. ■ This study shifts kids' attention away from an obsession with their temporal physical bodies toward something of eternal importance: spiritual growth

THE POINT:

Spiritual fitness is more important than physical fitness.

The Study
AT A GLANCE

SECTION	MINUTES	WHAT STUDENTS WILL DO	SUPPLIES
The Warm-Up	5 to 10	THE TRAINING ROOM—Perform exercises, discuss fitness, and then evaluate a quote from a famous athlete.	
The Workout	10 to 15	CHALLENGE—Lift "weights" and study Scripture to explore how challenge contributes to fitness.	Bibles, "Challenge" section of the "Olympic Rings" handout (p. 55), pencils, makeshift weights
	15 to 20	PERSEVERANCE—Act out the traits of good coaches and explore Scripture to learn about perseverance.	Bibles, "Perseverance" section of the "Olympic Rings" handout (p. 55), tape, pencils
The Cool Down	15 to 20	EXERCISE—List positive traits of physical and spiritual "athletes" and commit to spiritual exercise.	Bibles, "Exercise" section of the "Olympic Rings" handout (p. 55), index cards, tape, pencils

notes:

THE POINT OF *THE TOTAL PACKAGE:*

Spiritual fitness is more important than physical fitness.

THE BIBLE CONNECTION

HEBREWS 11:17–12:11	The author lists heroes of faith and uses athletic imagery to inspire spiritual growth.
PSALMS 119:11, 97-101; 143:5; MARK 1:35; LUKE 2:36-38; and ACTS 17:11	These passages contain examples of spiritual "exercises."

I n this study, kids will exercise their bodies, role play examples of good coaching, and study biblical heroes to explore the similarities and differences of physical and spiritual development. They'll learn three key components needed for both physical and spiritual exercise and will learn about and commit to doing spiritual "exercises."

Through these activities, kids can discover that to grow spiritually, they need to exercise spiritually. By exploring parallels between working out physically and working out spiritually, kids can understand that physical fitness cannot address their spiritual needs and can learn what to do to grow spiritually.

Explore the verses in The Bible Connection; then examine the information in the Depthfinder boxes throughout the study to gain a deeper understanding of how these Scriptures connect with your young people.

BEFORE THE STUDY

Before class, make one photocopy of the "Olympic Rings" handout (p. 55) for every student. Cut each copy into three sections along the dotted lines.

LEADER TIP for The Study

Junior highers can be extremely sensitive about their bodies. Throughout the study, be aware of your kids' needs; don't push them to do more than they can handle, and don't make anyone feel bad about his or her body. Be sure to circulate among the kids, affirming them for a variety of their good qualities instead of focusing on physical achievements.

THE STUDY

THE WARM-UP ▼

The Training Room (5 to 10 minutes) As the kids arrive, send the girls to one side of the room and the guys to the other side. Tell them that today's class is going to be about fitness so they'd better warm up and stretch out for the upcoming workout.

Once everyone has arrived, have kids perform the following exercises:

● Leg lifts: Lay flat on your back, put your legs together, and raise them six inches off the ground. Hold them there as long as you can.

● Abdominal crunches: Lay flat on your back with your arms across your chest. Bend your knees, and put your feet flat on the floor so you're in position to do sit-ups. Lift your upper body so your elbows touch your thighs. Hold that position as long as you can.

● Push-ups: Lay on your stomach with your arms bent so your hands are lying next to your shoulders. Keeping your body straight and stiff, push up with your arms. Then lower yourself halfway so your elbows are bent at a ninety-degree angle, and hold yourself there as long as you can.

After kids perform the exercises, regroup to discuss the following questions:

● **What would you have to do in order to condition yourself to do each of these exercises for five minutes straight?**

● **What makes a person a good, fit athlete?**

● **Do you think your spiritual heart needs the same kind of workout as your physical heart? Why or why not?**

● **What would characterize a good, fit "spiritual athlete"?**

Say: **Here's a quote from a famous athlete who's very physically fit—and wealthy. As I read the quote, think about whether the quote portrays spiritual fitness. Also think about the differences between physical fitness and spiritual fitness.** Read the following quote to the class:

"Right now I have to keep striving, striving, striving to be satisfied; just looking for that one element that's going to keep me happy at all times…For some reason I have no time to get happy. I think when I'm most happiest is when I'm actually so tense, so angry, so mad and disgusted, and I can relieve all that and be happy" (Dennis Rodman, quoted in Rolling Stone, December 12, 1996).

Ask the kids whether they think the quote portrays spiritual fitness. Then tell kids that the quote was from Dennis Rodman, a famous basketball player. Encourage discussion about the differences between physical fitness and spiritual fitness.

Then ask:

● **Some of the most physically fit, beautiful, wealthy people have**

ended their own lives—Marilyn Monroe, for example. **What do you think could be missing in the way these people view the world?**

Say: **Today we're going to talk about three components that help a person become more fit. Our society tells us it's very important to be physically fit and to look good. But when we look at the lives of some physically fit or beautiful people, we find that appearance doesn't make a person whole. What our society doesn't always make clear is that <u>spiritual fitness is more important than physical fitness.</u>**

LEADER TIP for The Training Room

If kids in your group aren't familiar with Dennis Rodman, use this background information during the discussion to lend insight into physical fitness and spiritual fitness. Dennis Rodman is a basketball player for the National Basketball Association and is regarded by many as the best rebounder in the league. The product of a rough upbringing, his on-court behavior sometimes mirrors the streets on which he played as a child. Rodman is known for his many tattoos, for his always-changing hair color, and for his in-your-face attitude both on and off the court. For kicking a court-side cameraman during a game, he was handed the second stiffest suspension and fine in the league's history. Rodman's nickname is "The Worm."

THE WORKOUT ▼

Challenge (10 to 15 minutes)

Have kids form groups of three or four. Give each group a light weight and a heavy weight. You can use what's available: pencils, chairs, benches, books. Have each student lift each of his or her group's "weight" ten to fifteen times. If you use heavier objects, have kids "spot" each other by helping to lift the weight.

After students have had a chance to lift weights, hand out a photocopy of the "Challenge" section of the "Olympic Rings" handout (p. 55) to each person. Give the groups five to ten minutes to work their way through this portion of the handout.

Perseverance (15 to 20 minutes)

Give each person one photocopy of the "Perseverance" section of the "Olympic Rings" handout (p. 55) and some tape, and have kids tape the "Perseverance" sections to their "Challenge" sections. Tell kids to turn the handout over and draw a horizontal line across the middle of the "Perseverance" section, dividing it in half. Then tell kids to label the top left-hand side, "My Ideal Coach." Then have them label the top right-hand side, "What It Will Be Like." You may want to draw this out before class to show it as an example to the students.

Ask kids to list the characteristics and responsibilities of a good coach under the left-hand column entitled "My Ideal Coach." To help them get started, ask:

● **What will this coach make you do?**
● **What is he or she like? tough? a pushover? a disciplinarian?**

Then under the column heading "What It Will Be Like," have kids list the good and bad consequences of training and playing under their ideal coach. To help them get started, ask:

● **Will you have sore muscles? injuries?**
● **Will there be a degree of suffering on the court?**
● **Will you have a winning season? Will there be some losses?**

Once they have generated their lists, give each group two minutes to prepare a thirty-second skit that highlights the items on group members' lists. Tell groups to include both the coach and player roles in their skits. After two minutes ask each group to act out its skit for the class.

LEADER TIP
for The Study

Whenever you tell groups to discuss a list of questions, write the list on newsprint and tape the newsprint to a wall so groups can answer the questions at their own pace.

LEADER TIP
for The Study

As kids work on each section of their handouts, circulate among the groups to provide assistance, insight, direction, and supervision.

DEPTHFINDER — UNDERSTANDING THE BIBLE

The book of Hebrews was written primarily to Jews who had converted to Christianity. They were facing persecution from both Romans and Jews and were starting to doubt the truth of Christ—perhaps even considering a return to Judaism. "Hence the urgency with which the author exhorts them, using a variety of metaphors, not to drift downstream but to row hard against the current, not to flag in the race but to persevere in faith" (The Zondervan Pictorial Encyclopedia of the Bible).

To encourage the Hebrews to remain faithful and to persevere, the author lists heroes of faith from the Old Testament—heroes his audience would be familiar with and would be inspired by. "If [Christians] were being persecuted, they would have the same temptation to opt for the easier way out. But no, they must have 'endurance' and 'faith', and the classic examples of this faith were all those great figures in the history of the Jewish race who had unswervingly adhered to the will of God in the face of all the discouragements that materialistic common sense or ruthless enemies could devise" (The New English Bible Companion to the New Testament).

Then in Hebrews 12, these heroes of faith "become a dense crowd of spectators seated round a stadium, while the athlete throws off every encumbrance and stands straining at the starting line, inspired by the example of one who has run the race with surpassing resolution: Jesus" (The New English Bible Companion to the New Testament). When the race is tiring, the author implores the Hebrews to "hold on through your sufferings, because they are like a father's discipline. God is treating you as children. All children are disciplined by their fathers" (Hebrews 12:7).

The author has provided a blueprint for spiritual exercise. Doubts may filter into our hearts. Hardship and struggles may weaken our faith. Waiting for Christ's return may tire us. But by living with faith and perseverance, by focusing on Jesus, and by responding to God's discipline, we can grow spiritually. And by growing spiritually, we can "run the race that is before us and never give up."

After groups have performed their skits, instruct the class to get their handouts, turn them to the back again, and label the bottom left-hand side, "God as a Coach" and the bottom right-hand side, "What It Will Be Like." Then have the kids turn their handouts over and follow the instructions under the "Perseverance" section.

After they have completed their lists, have kids discuss the following questions:

● **How is your ideal coach similar to God as a coach? How are they different?**

● **When you look at the columns "What It Will Be Like," how is spiritual training similar to physical training? How is it different?**

● **Why is it necessary to persevere through discipline?**

● **Can you become either spiritually or physically fit without persevering through strenuous hardship? If so, how would you get fit?**

● **How does it change things to think of God not only as our coach but also as our father?**

Then say: **To be truly fit, we have to understand that spiritual fitness is more important than physical fitness.** And the only way to get fit, either spiritually or physically, is to persevere

DEPTHFINDER
UNDERSTANDING ATHLETIC IMAGERY

Most teenagers understand the world of physical fitness, so studying parallels between physical fitness and spiritual fitness can help kids better understand how to become more spiritually fit.

The author of Hebrews uses athletic imagery to help his readers understand the work behind living a "fit" Christian life. To more fully appreciate that imagery, read the allegory below with the "Understanding the Bible" Depthfinder (p. 52). To help your students understand the athletic imagery in Hebrews 12:1-11, you may also want to read the allegory to your students.

Christian jogs in place. It's the race of his lifetime. The stadium is filled with all of his heroes, from the ancient ones to present-day Hall-of-Famers. These great competitors have deeply inspired him, just as they have inspired thousands of people for generations.

These heroes exhibited immense perseverance and discipline in training. Despite hardships and setbacks, they believed they would someday triumph over adversity. Like them, Christian knows about discipline. His coach has him on a strict diet, makes him practice an extra hour for every minute he's late, and even imposes a sleep quota on the weekends. It's not always pleasant. Sometimes it's painful. But Christian respects his coach; his coach is like a father. Besides, Christian knows the discipline is for his own good.

Christian remembers his coach's instruction to focus on him. Christian's coach also inspires him, and as Christian places his feet on the starting line, his legs feel strong and eager. He followed his coach, and he trained with discipline and perseverance just as his heroes did. Christian is ready for this race.

through the challenges that come our way. A challenge doesn't do us any good if we bail out midstream. Spiritual muscles are developed in the same way as physical muscles: by a patient and steadfast effort. But to be ready for the challenges, we have to do the right exercises.

THE COOL DOWN ▼

Exercise (15 to 20 minutes)
Give each person an index card, some tape, and one copy of the "Exercise" section of the "Olympic Rings" handout (p. 55). Have kids tape the "Exercise" section to the other sections. On the front of the index card, have each person write down the name of an athlete they respect. It can be a professional athlete, someone at school, or someone they know. On the back of the index card, have each person list admirable internal character traits of that athlete—for example, "hard worker," "disciplined," or "good sport." Steer kids away from listing external results of such traits—"best rebounder" or "big scorer," for example.

Then instruct everyone to find a classmate who also shows one of those traits and tape the index card on his or her back, with the trait facing out. There should be one card for each person.

LEADER TIP
for Exercise

If you're running short on time, have kids look up only two or three of the Scriptures listed on their handouts. Or assign a different Scripture to each group, and have each group report what it discovered to the rest of the class.

Before the students put together their personal exercise plans, create a reflective environment in the classroom. You may want to let them spread out to be alone for a few minutes. Encourage silence or play soft, worshipful music.

Then say: **Most of us know of athletes we admire and look up to. And usually those people don't earn our full respect unless they've worked really hard at all the right exercises. It's important to have spiritual role models as well who can show us the exercises that will make us spiritually fit.**

Have the students get back into their groups and follow the instructions on the "Exercise" section of their handouts. After kids have completed the section, encourage them to put their personal exercise plan into practice during the week.

Say: **As you discovered, there are very different exercises for spiritual fitness. Physical exercise won't ever get your spiritual heart in shape. You can look fit on the outside but be weak on the inside where it really counts. To be totally fit, you should understand that** <u>spiritual fitness is more important than physical fitness.</u>

Close in prayer, asking God to help the class grow in intimacy with Jesus so they can develop "spiritual muscle."

DEPTH FINDER — UNDERSTANDING SPIRITUAL DISCIPLINE

"**T**en Easy Ways to Trim Your Tummy!" "Lose Thirty Pounds in Two Weeks!" These kinds of titles and headlines permeate our society, and kids internalize them. Our fast-food, instant culture likes to find the quickest, least painful way to ascend the throne of perfection. The truth is that nothing worthwhile comes easy. There are few honest "get rich quick" schemes in life. Magic formulas for physical perfection are as mythological as Hercules himself.

Nothing replaces "old-fashioned" virtues such as patience, commitment, discipline, challenge, and perseverance. Physical fitness doesn't come easy, and spiritual fitness is no different. Encourage kids to see the spiritual disciplines as just that: worthwhile discipline. Help kids realize that spiritual growth requires discipline but that the discipline doesn't take the joy out of life with God.

Olympic Rings

Challenge

After lifting the two weights, discuss these questions:
- If you wanted to develop strength, which weight would you use? Why?
- What would happen if there was never any challenge?

Read Hebrews 11:17-40. List the many situations that challenged the faith of these real people on the back of this handout. Then discuss the following questions:
- What is the writer of Hebrews commending these people for?
- What do you suppose happened to them when they were challenged?
- What challenging situations do you face that stretch your faith?
- What are ways that you can challenge yourself in order to gain spiritual muscle?
- How can you motivate yourself to persevere through difficulties?

- -

Perseverance

Read Hebrews 12:4-11. As you read, list everything it says about God on the back side of this paper under "God as a Coach." What is he compared to? What does he do?

Then under "What It Will Be Like," list what the Bible says it's like to be under God's coaching. Are there unpleasant consequences? What will the good consequences be?

- -

Exercise

Read Hebrews 12:1-3. Then discuss the following questions:
- In these verses, who are the "many people whose lives tell us what faith means"?
- Which of those people do you admire as a spiritual role model? Why?

The passage encourages us to look to Jesus as our principal role model because of the way he persevered through all the hard challenges in his life. He did the right spiritual "exercises" to be prepared for the challenges, as did the many people referred to in Hebrews 12:1. Read the following Scriptures, and write down the spiritual exercises these role models did to get in spiritual shape. Then list any additional exercises you can think of.

- Mark 1:35

- Luke 2:36-38

- Psalm 119:11, 97-101

- Psalm 143:5

- Acts 17:11

Put together a spiritual training plan for yourself by answering the questions below on the back of your handout.

- What are two things that hinder me from getting to know my role model, Jesus, better?
- What are two ways I can stay motivated to avoid mediocrity?
- What two challenges or trials am I currently facing, and how can I persevere through them?
- The two spiritual exercises I will do this week in order to accomplish the above and bring me closer to Jesus are…

why ▼Active and Interactive Learning works with teenagers

Let's Start With the Big Picture

Think back to a major life lesson you've learned.
Got it? Now answer these questions:

● Did you learn your lesson from something you read?
● Did you learn it from something you heard?
● Did you learn it from something you experienced?

If you're like 99 percent of your peers, you answered "yes" only to the third question—you learned your life lesson from something you experienced.

This simple test illustrates the most convincing reason for using active and interactive learning with young people: People learn best through experience. Or to put it even more simply, people learn by doing.

Learning by doing is what active learning is all about. No more sitting quietly in chairs and listening to a speaker expound theories about God—that's passive learning. Active learning gets kids out of their chairs and into the experience of life. With active learning, kids get to *do* what they're studying. They *feel* the effects of the principles you teach. They *learn* by experiencing truth firsthand.

Active learning works because it recognizes three basic learning needs and uses them in concert to enable young people to make discoveries on their own and to find practical life applications for the truths they believe.

So what are these three basic learning needs?

1. Teenagers need action.
2. Teenagers need to think.
3. Teenagers need to talk.

Read on to find out exactly how these needs will be met by using the active and interactive learning techniques in Group's Core Belief Bible Study Series in your youth group.

1. Teenagers Need Action

Aircraft pilots know well the difference between passive and active learning. Their passive learning comes through listening to flight instructors and reading flight-instruction books. Their active learning comes through actually flying an airplane or flight simulator. Books and lectures may be helpful, but pilots really learn to fly by manipulating a plane's controls themselves.

We can help young people learn in a similar way. Though we may engage students passively in some reading and listening to teachers, their understanding and application of God's Word will really take off through simulated and real-life experiences.

Forms of active learning include simulation games; role-plays; service projects; experiments; research projects; group pantomimes; mock trials; construction projects; purposeful games; field trips; and, of course, the most powerful form of active learning—real-life experiences.

We can more fully explain active learning by exploring four of its characteristics:

● **Active learning is an adventure.** Passive learning is almost always predictable. Students sit passively while the teacher or speaker follows a planned outline or script.

In active learning, kids may learn lessons the teacher never envisioned. Because the leader trusts students to help create the learning experience, learners may venture into unforeseen discoveries. And often the teacher learns as much as the students.

● **Active learning is fun and captivating.** What are we communicating when we say, "OK, the fun's over—time to talk about God"? What's the hidden message? That joy is separate from God? And that learning is separate from joy?

What a shame.

Active learning is not joyless. One seventh-grader we interviewed clearly remembered her best Sunday school lesson: "Jesus was the light, and we went into a dark room and shut off the lights. We had a candle, and we learned that Jesus is the light and the dark can't shut off the light." That's active learning. Deena enjoyed the lesson. She had fun. And she learned.

Active learning intrigues people. Whether they find a foot-washing experience captivating or maybe a bit uncomfortable, they learn. And they learn on a level deeper than any work sheet or teacher's lecture could ever reach.

● **Active learning involves everyone.** Here the difference between passive and active learning becomes abundantly clear. It's like the difference between watching a football game on television and actually playing in the game.

The "trust walk" provides a good example of involving everyone in active learning. Half of the group members put on blindfolds; the other half serve as guides. The "blind" people trust the guides to lead them through the building or outdoors. The guides prevent the blind people from falling down stairs or tripping over rocks. Everyone needs to participate to learn the inherent lessons of trust, faith, doubt, fear, confidence, and servanthood. Passive spectators of this experience would learn little, but participants learn a great deal.

● **Active learning is focused through debriefing.** Activity simply for activity's sake doesn't usually result in good learning. Debriefing—evaluating an experience by discussing it in pairs or small groups—helps focus the experience and draw out its meaning. Debriefing helps sort and order the information students gather during the experience. It helps learners relate the recently experienced activity to their lives.

The process of debriefing is best started immediately after an experience. We use a three-step process in debriefing: reflection, interpretation, and application.

Reflection—This first step asks the students, "How did you feel?" Active-learning experiences typically evoke an emotional reaction, so it's appropriate to begin debriefing at that level.

Some people ask, "What do feelings have to do with education?" Feelings have everything to do with education. Think back again to that time in your life when you learned a big lesson. In all likelihood, strong feelings accompanied that lesson. Our emotions tend to cement things into our memories.

When you're debriefing, use open-ended questions to probe feelings. Avoid questions that can be answered with a "yes" or "no." Let your learners know that there are no wrong answers to these "feeling" questions. Everyone's feelings are valid.

Interpretation—The next step in the debriefing process asks, "What does this mean to you? How is this experience like or unlike some other aspect of your life?" Now you're asking people to identify a message or principle from the experience.

You want your learners to discover the message for themselves. So instead of telling students your answers, take the time to ask questions that encourage self-discovery. Use Scripture and discussion in pairs or small groups to explore how the actions and effects of the activity might translate to their lives.

Alert! Some of your people may interpret wonderful messages that you never intended. That's not failure! That's the Holy Spirit at work. God allows us to catch different glimpses of his kingdom even when we all look through the same glass.

Application—The final debriefing step asks, "What will you do about it?" This step moves learning into action. Your young people have shared a common experience. They've discovered a principle. Now they must create something new with what they've just experienced and interpreted. They must integrate the message into their lives.

The application stage of debriefing calls for a decision. Ask your students how they'll change, how they'll grow, what they'll do as a result of your time together.

2. Teenagers Need to Think

Today's students have been trained not to think. They aren't dumber than previous generations. We've simply conditioned them not to use their heads.

You see, we've trained our kids to respond with the simplistic answers they think the teacher wants to hear. Fill-in-the-blank student workbooks and teachers who ask dead-end questions such as "What's the capital of Delaware?" have produced kids and adults who have learned not to think.

And it doesn't just happen in junior high or high school. Our children are schooled very early not to think. Teachers attempt to help kids read with nonsensical fill-in-the-blank drills, word scrambles, and missing-letter puzzles.

Helping teenagers think requires a paradigm shift in how we teach. We need to plan for and set aside time for higher-order thinking and be willing to reduce our time spent on lower-order parroting. Group's Core Belief Bible Study Series is designed to help you do just that.

Thinking classrooms look quite different from traditional classrooms. In most church environments, the teacher does most of the talking and hopes that knowledge will transmit from his or her brain to the students'. In thinking settings, the teacher coaches students to ponder, wonder, imagine, and problem-solve.

3. Teenagers Need to Talk

Everyone knows that the person who learns the most in any class is the teacher. Explaining a concept to someone else is usually more helpful to the explainer than to the listener. So why not let the students do more teaching? That's one of the chief benefits of letting kids do the talking. This process is called interactive learning.

What is interactive learning? Interactive learning occurs when students discuss and work cooperatively in pairs or small groups.

Interactive learning encourages learners to work together. It honors the fact that students can learn from one another, not just from the teacher. Students work together in pairs or small groups to accomplish shared goals. They build together, discuss together, and present together. They teach each other and learn from one another. Success as a group is celebrated. Positive interdependence promotes individual and group learning.

Interactive learning not only helps people learn but also helps learners feel better about themselves and get along better with others. It accomplishes these things more effectively than the independent or competitive methods.

Here's a selection of interactive learning techniques that are used in Group's Core Belief Bible Study Series. With any of these models, leaders may assign students to specific partners or small groups. This will maximize cooperation and learning by preventing all the "rowdies" from linking up. And it will allow for new friendships to form outside of established cliques.

Following any period of partner or small-group work, the leader may reconvene the entire class for large-group processing. During this time the teacher may ask for reports or discoveries from individuals or teams. This technique builds in accountability for the teacherless pairs and small groups.

Pair-Share—With this technique each student turns to a partner and responds to a question or problem from the teacher or leader. Every learner responds. There are no passive observers. The teacher may then ask people to share their partners' responses.

Study Partners—Most curricula and most teachers call for Scripture passages to be read to the whole class by one person. One reads; the others doze.

Why not relinquish some teacher control and let partners read and react with each other? They'll all be involved—and will learn more.

Learning Groups—Students work together in small groups to create a model, design artwork, or study a passage or story; then they discuss what they learned through the experience. Each person in the learning group may be assigned a specific role. Here are some examples:

Reader

Recorder (makes notes of key thoughts expressed during the reading or discussion)

Checker (makes sure everyone understands and agrees with answers arrived at by the group)

Encourager (urges silent members to share their thoughts)

When everyone has a specific responsibility, knows what it is, and contributes to a small group, much is accomplished and much is learned.

Summary Partners—One student reads a paragraph, then the partner summarizes the paragraph or interprets its meaning. Partners alternate roles with each paragraph.

The paraphrasing technique also works well in discussions. Anyone who wishes to share a thought must first paraphrase what the previous person said. This sharpens listening skills and demonstrates the power of feedback communication.

Jigsaw—Each person in a small group examines a different concept, Scripture, or part of an issue. Then each teaches the others in the group. Thus, all members teach, and all must learn the others' discoveries. This technique is called a jigsaw because individuals are responsible to their group for different pieces of the puzzle.

JIGSAW EXAMPLE

Here's an example of a jigsaw.

Assign four-person teams. Have teammates each number off from one to four. Have all the Ones go to one corner of the room, all the Twos to another corner, and so on.

Tell team members they're responsible for learning information in their numbered corners and then for teaching their team members when they return to their original teams.

Give the following assignments to various groups:

Ones: Read Psalm 22. Discuss and list the prophecies made about Jesus.

Twos: Read Isaiah 52:13–53:12. Discuss and list the prophecies made about Jesus.

Threes: Read Matthew 27:1-32. Discuss and list the things that happened to Jesus.

Fours: Read Matthew 27:33-66. Discuss and list the things that happened to Jesus.

After the corner groups meet and discuss, instruct all learners to return to their original teams and report what they've learned. Then have each team determine which prophecies about Jesus were fulfilled in the passages from Matthew.

Call on various individuals in each team to report one or two prophecies that were fulfilled.

You Can Do It Too!

All this information may sound revolutionary to you, but it's really not. God has been using active and interactive learning to teach his people for generations. Just look at Abraham and Isaac, Jacob and Esau, Moses and the Israelites, Ruth and Boaz. And then there's Jesus, who used active learning all the time!

Group's Core Belief Bible Study Series makes it easy for you to use active and interactive learning with your group. The active and interactive elements are automatically built in! Just follow the outlines, and watch as your kids grow through experience and positive interaction with others.

FOR DEEPER STUDY

For more information on incorporating active and interactive learning into your work with teenagers, check out these resources:

● *Why Nobody Learns Much of Anything at Church: And How to Fix It,* by Thom and Joani Schultz (Group Publishing) and
● *Do It! Active Learning in Youth Ministry,* by Thom and Joani Schultz (Group Publishing).

your evaluation of

Bible Study Series
for junior high/middle school

the truth about
SPIRITUAL GROWTH

Group Publishing, Inc.
Attention: Core Belief Talk-Back
P.O. Box 481
Loveland, CO 80539
Fax: (970) 669-1994

Please help us continue to provide innovative and useful resources for ministry. After you've led the studies in this volume, take a moment to fill out this evaluation; then mail or fax it to us at the address above. Thanks!

● ● ● ● ● ●

1. As a whole, this book has been (circle one)

not very helpful   very helpful
1   2   3   4   5   6   7   8   9   10

2. The best things about this book:

3. How this book could be improved:

4. What I will change because of this book:

5. Would you be interested in field-testing future Core Belief Bible Studies and giving us your feedback? If so, please complete the information below:

Name _____

Street address _____

City _____ State _____Zip _____

Daytime telephone (____) _____ Date _____

THANKS!